Poetry to God,
Volume 1

Lord, Please Hear the Cry

TERRY WEBB

Order this book online at _www.amazon.com_ (http://www.amazon.com)
or my personal website: poetrytogod.org
or at any other retailer

Copyright 2011 Terry Webb
All rights reserved. No part of this publication may be reproduced, stored in a retrieval
system, or transmitted, in any form or by any means, electric, mechanical, photocopying,
recording, or otherwise, without the written prior permission of the author Terry Webb.

Printed in the United States of America.

ISBN: 978-0-6157-3303-6

Library of Congress Control Number: 2011901030

To my father God:

I thank you my Heavenly Father, For keeping me focused and giving me strength to follow my dreams as a poet/writer.
I thank you for your spirit and character showing me the way.
I am forever grateful.

I am grateful for my imagination. I will be open to having faith in all possibilities.

I am grateful being a part of your creation and being chosen to write your book *"POETRY TO GOD"*

SPECIAL DEDICATION

Special Thanks to my mother "Cora Webb" for her unconditional never ending love for me and to my wife Sharon Webb and all of my son's and daughters for their love and support. Robert Webb, Ziarion Webb, Perry Webb, Latisia Webb, La Shondra Webb and Adrian Jackson, and my grand children Michelle Mosley, Danisha Webb, Diamond Webb, Robert Webb Jr. December Webb, Sharon Foster, Keashon Foster.

Special Thanks to Shawn Rahimi "my boss" Velma Moss, Mamie Foster and Erica Marquez "my co workers" at "General Discount" Los Angeles, Calif. for ever reminding me to continue writing, follow my dream and to keep my faith in God.

Special Thanks to all my friends that gave me words of encouragement and that little extra touch of love that helped me get my life back on track when I was lost in the world. And to Sabrina Moultrie for entering my poem "BELIEVE IN HIM" in a poetry contest and winning, I thank you all so much, God loves you and so do I . . .

A Very Special Thanks to Betty Bynum and Antwone Fisher for their privilege of allowing me to recite my poem "LORD, PLEASE HEAR THE CRY" at the "POETRY OF ANTWONE FISHER" PEACE4KIDS EVENT PRODUCED BY: WORK HOUSE ROAD PRODUCTIONS.

I love you all and truly thank God for all of you being a part of my life . . .

Sincerely Yours
TERRY WEBB

FOREWORD

Throughout my life, I've stored information collected from experiences and try in some way to make sense of it. When I am not able to fully understand the things that occur in my life, I take time to process the information. By doing this, I am afforded a different perspective, thus allowing me to think more clearly about difficult or perplexing events and emotions, Poetry is a way in which I choose to externalize my thoughts.

Poetry is a very powerful tool by which I can share sometimes confusing, sometimes perfectly clear concepts and feelings with others. All I simply want is to share in poetic form, something that has touched my life in some way to others. Some of my poems may speak to the hearts of certain readers more than others, but keep in mind that each poem is my voice, of my mind that needs to make sense of this world, of my heart that feels the effects of every moment in this life, of my heart striving to have a closer walk with GOD.

TABLE OF CONTENTS

LORD, PLEASE HEAR THE CRY	1
"THE DREAM"	3
"VICTORY"	5
"BRIDGE TO PARADISE"	6
"FOR YOU I DIED"	7
"THE RIVER OF LIFE"	8
"I WONDER WHY?"	9
"THE MIRROR"	10
"IF JESUS COMES TODAY"	11
"A HEART AFLAME"	12
"BELIEVE"	13
BELIEVE IN HIM	14
BLESSED LORD	15
"CALL TO WORSHIP"	16
"CHILDREN OF LIGHT"	17
"DOES ANYONE CARE ANYMORE"	18
"EVER PRESENT LOVE"	19
"FIRST SEEK GOD"	20
"FAITHFUL TO END"	21
"SIMPLE TASK #1"	22
GIVE LOVE AWAY	23
"I GIVE YOU JESUS"	24
"I AM"	25
"THANK YOU LORD"	26
TAKE COVER, CHILD	27
"THE ANGEL OF DEATH"	28
"STUBBORN CHILD"	29
"SHARE MY SORROW"	30
"REAP THE HARVEST"	31

PRECIOUS LOVE	32
"LEAD ME TO HEAVEN"	33
"HIS LOVE FOREVER"	34
"HE IS CALLING YOUR NAME"	35
"HE IS!"	36
"HE HAS PROMISED"	37
"GRACE IS FOUND"	38
"GOD THE CREATOR!"	39
"JESUS" YOU TOLD ME	40
"NEVER A TEARDROP"	41
"MY LIFE TO JESUS"	42
"WHO AM I"	43
"WALK WITH GOD"	44
YOU ARE MY STRENGTH "EACH DAY"	45
"O" LUCIFER	46
"A GREAT LOVE"	47
"MY HEART'S DESIRE"	48
"I'LL BE WITH YOU"	49
HIS GREAT SURPRISE	50
"ACCEPT CHRIST NOW"	51
"CLEANSE ME LORD"	52
GROW TO KNOW JESUS	53
"HIS LIFE FOR OURS"	54
"WISDOM"	55
"ALL PRAISE THE KING"	56
BE NOT DISMAYED	57
"CHRIST PAID"	58
FOREVER THE SAME	59
"THE RISEN LORD"	60
"BE NOT AFRAID"	61
"I SHALL WAIT"	62
"AWESOME GOD"	63
"BEHOLD, YOUR KING"	64
"CHANGED WITHIN"	65
"DOING GODS WILL"	66
"EVERY IDLE WORD"	67

FOLLOW ME	68
FATHER IN HEAVEN	69
"SIMPLE TASK 2"	70
GOD IS	71
"I AM WITH YOU"	72
"TEACH YOUR CHILD"	73
SURPRISE WITHIN MY EYES	74
"REFLECTIONS"	75
PRAYER OF PROTECTION	76
LIVING WATER	77
"HIS STAR"	78
"HE IS SO WONDERFUL"	79
"HE IS NEVER TO BUSY"	80
GOD WILL SUPPLY	81
"JESUS AND ME"	82
"NO NEED FOR LIGHT"	83
"MY EVERYTHING"	84
"WHO IS HE?"	85
"WHAT JESUS REALLY WANTS"	86
"YOU GIVE"	87
"O" PRECIOUS LAMB	88
"BUT ONCE"	89
I'M JESUS "REMEMBER ME"	90
"HALLOWED BE HIS NAME"	91
"A WISHFUL PRAYER"	92
"CLOCK OF LIFE"	93
TRIALS	94
"SINS REMEDY"	95
"WITH HIS HANDS"	96
ALL IS GOD'S	97
"CHRIST PAID THE PRICE"	98
"DEVOTION"	99
FOREVER TRUE	100
"I SURRENDER"	101
THIS TELLS ME	102
"ALWAYS"	103

"BEAUTY IN YOU" 104
"CHILD OF GOD" 105
"DON'T GIVE UP" 106
"EVERYONE DREAMS" 107
"FOLLOW THE STAR" 108
"FEAR NOT" 109
"SIMPLE TASK 3" 110
"GOD" 111
"I NEED THE LORD" 112
THE BIBLE 113
"SURRENDER TO HIS LOVE" 114
"RIVER OF LIFE" 115
"LIFE AFTER DEATH" 116
"HEAVENLY WISDOM" 117
"HE IS WORTHY" 118
"GOD'S UNCONDITIONAL LOVE" 119
"JESUS IS HE" 120
NO NEED TO HIDE 121
MY PERFECT LOVE 122
"WHERE IS YOUR TREASURE" 123
"YOU NEED JESUS" 124
"ON BENDED KNEE" 125
"CONFESS YOUR SINS" 126
"IN HARMONY WITH GOD" 127
"GRATITUDE" 128
"A PURE HEART" 129
"COME HOME" 130
"GODS WORD" 131
THE HEAVENS GLORY OF GOD 132
"WITH JESUS" 133
"ALL HAVE SINNED" 134
BE A STAR 135
"CHRISTLIKE WITH LOVE" 136
"DRY THY EYE" 137
FUTURE VIEW 138
"FORGIVEN" 139

"I SURRENDER ALL"	140
"THY GRACE"	141
"ALL TRUST IN YOU"	142
"BE THE LIGHT"	143
"CHOSEN FOR HIS GLORY"	144
"DON'T LOOK BEHIND"	145
"EYES OF FAITH"	146
"FOOTPRINTS OF JESUS"	147
"FEED MY SHEEP"	148
"SIMPLE TASK 4"	149
"GOD IS ALRIGHT"	150
"I REPENT"	151
"THE BLOOD"	152
"SPIRITUAL STRENGTH"	153
"SALVATION"	154
LIGHT OF MY LIFE	155
"HOLY SPIRIT"	156
"HE'S ALL I NEED"	157
HELP ME KNOW YOU	158
"GOD'S GREATNESS IS SEEN"	159
"JESUS IS LORD"	160
"NO ONE'S PERFECT"	161
"MY FUTURE"	162
YOU'RE NEVER ALONE	163
"ONCE TO DIE"	164
"COME UNTO ME"	165
INDIVIDUALLY MADE	166
"NOT MINE OWN"	167
"A PROMISE OF COMFORT"	168
COME TO ME	169
"TIME OUT FOR GOD"	170
"I SEEK THEE LORD"	171
"ALL ARE THE SAME"	172
"BROKEN LIVES"	173
"CHRIST'S RETURN"	174
"FROM HEAVEN WITH LOVE"	175

"I WILL PRAISE HIM"	176
THY PERFECT WILL	177
"ALL THINGS ARE POSSIBLE"	178
BE STRAIGHT WITH GOD	179
"CHRIST CARES"	180
DO YOU BELIEVE?	181
"FOR ALL I AM"	182
FIGHT THE GOOD FIGHT	183
"SIMPLE TASK 5"	184
"GOD ONLY KNOWS"	185
"I SEE GOD"	186
"THE EYES OF GOD"	187
SOMEDAY WE WILL BE TOGETHER	188
"SIMPLY TRUST"	189
LET GO—LET GOD	190
"HOW GREAT THOU ART"	191
"HIS GLORY"	192
"HE'S WAITING FOR YOU"	193
"GOD'S VESSEL"	194
"JESUS, PRINCE OF LOVE"	195
"NO OTHER NAME LIKE JESUS"	196
MY GOD, MY LORD	197
"WHY CALL ME LORD?"	198
"ONE LIFE TO LIVE"	199
"WHY IS CHRISTMAS"	200
"JESUS—KING OF KINGS"	201
"HOLY NIGHT"	202
"A GIFT FOR THE WORLD"	203
"STARLIGHTS OF THE NIGHT"	204
"SUMMER"	205
"WONDERS OF SPRING"	206
"MOTHER'S RECOGNITION"	207
"A MOTHER'S LOVE"	209
ABOUT THE AUTHOR	211
"MIRROR OF MY LIFE"	213

LORD, PLEASE HEAR THE CRY

People are fighting and killing,
All over the world, people die,
And no one is trying to stop,
Or help the people when they cry.
People only understand violence,
Seems nobody even care,
Because man's heart has turned to evil,
And love is no longer there.
Riots, stealing, killings and rape,
It's happening in every town,
People witness seeing these things
And they turn their heads around.
It's hard to even trust your neighbor,
Don't even turn your back,
Because the atmosphere in this world has,
Changed all people, White, Brown and Black.
Once, we were called "Brother,"
Together, we all shared fun,
But somehow, something changed the love,
We shared under the Sun.
Lord, look upon all men,
They call each other brother,
But they get involved in gangs and,
Drugs, then they kill one another.
Lord, look upon the children,
They are too young to understand,
The violence and the confusion,
And the hate in the heart of man.
For they are innocent and pure at heart,
Too young to even know,
What's happening in this corrupted world,
Or which direction they should go.
Bless the man who lost his job,
To take care of his family,
Bless him, Lord, and guide him,
And keep his heart with Thee.

Continued

Lord, look upon the homeless
Out there sleeping in the street,
People ignore and look down on them,
And they are lost, with nothing to eat.
If more people cared,
Enough to even give,
Just a little food or shelter,
Enough that they may live.
Lord, look upon the people walking,
Around like there's no hope,
For they are truly lost, because,
Their minds are filled with dope.
Bless the men in prison, Lord,
No longer they are free,
Bless them Lord, and guide them,
And bring them closer to Thee.
"O" Lord. please listen, please,
Listen to this cry!
Please look upon the tears of man,
And win their hearts before they die!

Written By: Terry Webb

"THE DREAM"

Last night as I lay in bed
This dream came unto me-
I dreamed about the end of time,
About eternity.
I dreamed I saw millions of sinners
Fall on their face to pray-
The Savior sadly shook his head,
And this I heard him say:
"Sorry I never knew you,
Go serve whom you served before
I'm sorry I never knew you,
For you I've closed the door."
I thought this was the time,
That I must stand before the trial-
So I told the Lord I was a Christian,
All my life long while.
But, through the book of life he looked,
And then he shook his head-
His Angels placed me to His left,
And then the Savior said:
"I'm sorry I never knew you,
I have no record of your birth.
Sorry, I never knew you,
Go serve your master on earth."
I then saw my wife and children,
I also heard each one's voice-
They all seemed very happy,
With joy, they did rejoice.
With robes of white around them all,
And crowns upon their head-
My youngest son, he looked at me,
And this is what he said . . .
"Daddy, we can't go with you,
We must stay upon this shore.
I'm sorry, but we still love you,
But you can't be daddy anymore."
Then from my sleep I did awake,
Tears were in my eyes-
Confused I looked around me,
Amazed with great surprise.

Continued

I saw my wife and all my sons,
Then knew it was a dream-
So down beside my bed I fell,
For God's mercy, I did scream,
"O" Father, whom art in Heaven,
In mercy, hear me today!
Forgive me and let me serve you, Lord
Until you call me away.
Please take my hand and guide my step,
Lord, save me from my sin-
Protect me from the evil one,
Also from sinful men.
Hear my prayer, I beg of Thee,
Give ear unto my cry!
"O" Lord, don't let that dream come true,
IN SIN, DON'T LET ME DIE!!!!!

By: TERRY WEBB

"VICTORY"

There is a victory over sin
Also over it's shame,
You'll find the victory in Jesus Christ
There's power in His name.

How can the devil pull you away
Or cause you to even sin,
When you belong to Christ the Lord
With Him, you'll always win.

Nothing can pull you from His hand
He will forever keep thy soul,
All the schemes, that Satan devise
The Lord, He will control.

As long as you're in step with Him
Living a life that's true,
You'll find that Jesus Christ the Lord
Will always be with you.

He purged your sins and paid your debt
That day at Calvary,
His life He gave, that you may live
In total, **"VICTORY."**

By Terry Webb

"BRIDGE TO PARADISE"

One night I dreamed I took a walk
Across a stretch of ground.
The ground was covered with rotted timber,
And junk was all around.

I was passing through what seemed to be
My life of sin and shame-
But, I kept on walking hopelessly,
With nothing in life to gain;

Then, just ahead I saw a bridge
Over a river sparkling blue;
And across this bridge I saw a meadow
With grass all anew.

Inside this meadow, I saw a man;
He was standing upon a hill;
His arms were reaching outward to me,
And He said, **"PEACE, BE STILL!"**

I knew not what to say to Him,
Nor, could I look upon His face,
Because I felt the presence of the Lord'
And the glory of His grace,

Then I knew this was the Son of God
Because His glory was divine,
And, He says to me, "Come on across
To Paradise, Thou Art Mine!"

By Terry Webb

"FOR YOU I DIED"

O Lord, you said that you would come-
And share with me my sorrow,
You told me Lord, that you'll be there-
For all of my tomorrow.

Out of my life, I pushed you back-
I tried to anyway,
But as you gave your Word to me-
I'm with you child to stay.

You lead me to the living waters-
And stood there by my side,
You knew my soul was thirsty Lord-
And my soul was not denied.

I cannot explain your love for me-
It's hard to understand,
How you accept me as I am-
A shameful sinner man.

For all my tears, you heard my cry-
How great thy love for me,
You loosed the chains, that had me bound-
In you now Lord I'm free.

I first was your's, then sin came in-
You heard me when I cried,
Then you said: **"That sin is why"**
"I gave my life and died!"

By Terry Webb

"THE RIVER OF LIFE"

Sparkling water as clear as crystals,
Flowing from my throne,
This water can be yours, my child,
If you would be mine own.

Just look to me through all your life-
Turn from the worlds delight,
The world can offer only death,
Treasures that allure thy sight.

"I offer life," to thee I'll give it,
Always abundantly;
"My arms are always open my child,"
"Come now unto me."

Let worldly minds the world pursue-
Don't live within it's pleasure,
"Come and look in faith to me,"
I offer greater treasure.

"I offer eternal life my child,"
From my throne do flow,
Living Waters, as clear as crystals-
This I tell you so.

So turn aside this wretched world-
Of brokenness and strife,
And come to Me, unto my throne,
"I am the River of Life."

By Terry Webb

"I WONDER WHY?"

I looked up to the sky, my mind wondered why,
Why all things are as they are, why did Jesus have to die?
I WONDERED WHY?
Then I gazed upon the stars, one twinkled to my eye,
All of a sudden, I started to cry,
I WONDERED WHY?
I wondered, why is a rich man rich, Why will he not help the poor?
Why do the ocean waves, dance to and from the shore?
I WONDERED WHY?
Why do man hunger, why does man steal?
Why does man get sick, and why do man kill?
I WONDERED WHY?
Why are there wars, blood shed and hell?
Why are there guns, policeman and jails?
I WONDERED WHY?
These things and more, is why Jesus had to die,
"Sin," is the reason, and the answer why!

By Terry Webb

"THE MIRROR"

Your face is a mirror, of the heart
Does Christ reflect from you?
Does He reflect in the way you live
Through all the things you do?

If people should enter your home today
Will the love of God be there?
If they even ask you about the Lord
Will you, God's Word then share?

Will the love of God reflect from you
As light, seen afar?
As the early morning's horizon sun
Or the bright and morning star?

What's in your heart? Is it love?
Or is there hate within?
What's in your heart, shows on your face
It shows if you're in sin.

Your face is a mirror, of your heart
So live a life that's true-
For whatever is deep within your heart
Will reflect outward on you!

By: TERRY WEBB

"IF JESUS COMES TODAY"

No one knows how long they have
Till their time is past,
So try and live your life each day
As if it were your last.

For when the Lord do returns
We do not want to be found,
Flirting or preoccupied, in this world
Sinning, round and round.

Our mind should be on Jesus Christ
The One in which we love,
Our lives will then be purified
By the love of Him above.

What if He comes for us today
Will you be ready to meet
The Lord our God, Jesus Christ
His coming you will greet?

We're not prepared to live until
We are prepared to die
Put away sin by the blood of Christ
Tell Satan he is a lie

Will you be found preoccupied-
In this world today?
Or will you be ready for his return-
If Jesus came today!

Written By: Terry Webb

"A HEART AFLAME"

Give to me Lord, a strong desire,
Please let my heart, burn like fire.
To spread Thy Word, each given day,
To help the wandering, find their way.
Please hide Thy Word, within my heart,
That I may keep it, and never part.
Lest from it's truth, my feet should stray,
And lead my soul, damnations way.
Thy Word, My heart, please let it glow,
Thy love, "O" Lord", please let it flow.
Let evil attract, no part of me,
Keep my eyes turned, only toward Thee.
Give me the will, to never rest,
Until my good, is better than best.
So when death comes, it's vale of shade,
I will look for thee Lord, and not be afraid.

By Terry Webb

"BELIEVE"

Believe that, "He who is coming, will come and will not delay"
Will come to judge a sinful world, on this judgment day,
Prepare your heart for His coming, carefully as you can prepare-
For He will surely come my friend, on a cloud high in the air.
Believe that His is coming, one day He will appear-
Believe that His is coming, that time is getting near.

By: TERRY WEBB

BELIEVE IN HIM

Where is your faith, "O" little one?
Do you not believe in God's only Son?
Do you not know that He died for you?
Simply because He deeply loves you.
You know, He gave His life upon a cross
For both you and I, for we were both lost.
He endured the hurting, agonizing pain;
Giving His life so that ours should remain.
Do you not believe that He did this for you?
Through all the pain that He went through.
Why do you not believe in God's only Son?
Woe unto you, "O" little one!

By Terry Webb

BLESSED LORD

Blessed is He, the Lord, my God
For He has showed me love.
Blessed is He, the Lord, my God
Whom reigns in heaven above.
"O" Lord, how great is Thy goodness
Which Thou has laid up for me.
Lord, God, how great is Thy goodness
for them, in which fear Thee.
Unconditional love He has for all,
And He looks upon all men.
Grace and hope is in His eyes
His mercy for those in sin.
taste and see that the Lord is good
All that are upright in heart.
The Lord truly rewards the faithful,
And His love for them never part.
Blessed is He, the Lord, My God
Merciful always is He
Blessed is He in the heavens,
"O" Lord, be not far from me.

By Terry Webb

"CALL TO WORSHIP"

We are called unto the Lord-
For worship day and night,
To worship Him and praise His name-
To do what's true and right.

We are created in His image-
For worship and for praise,
So we must praise His Holy Name-
All your life long day's.

There is no time of day or night-
No place on land or sea,
That God, whose ever watching eye-
Is unaware of thee.

Our lives we are to yield to Him-
His name we are to praise,
He say's to all with open hearts-
To praise His name always.

Now is the time to praise the Lord-
Praise Him while you may,
For tomorrow is not promised friend-
Worship Him Today.

By Terry Webb

"CHILDREN OF LIGHT"

Blessed are the children of light
Their lips and lives express,
One who walks and talks with God
The gospel they profess.

For they are called with Holy calling
A light they now must be,
Their lights must shine before all men
That they the light may see.

By them shall every person know
There is a God above,
His spirit dwells within their hearts
And fills them with his love.

Wherever they apply themselves
They're work is done with zest,
For what they do is for the Lord
And He Expects their best.

The works they do in Jesus name
God's only begotten Son,
Does bring much joy unto the Lord
With love they're works are done.

They are not afraid to do at all
What's good and what is right,
They're lives they live unto the Lord
As "Children of the light."

By Terry Webb

"DOES ANYONE CARE ANYMORE"

Does anyone care, in this world today?
Does anyone care, what the good Lord say?
Does anyone care, of the life they live?
Has everyone forgot, how to love and give?
Are there any hope, existing in the heart?
Or is everyone's heart, sinfully apart?
Does anyone care, about the next man?
Will he pass him by, or help if he can?
Is the whole world like, the rich standing tall?
Do they even hear, the poor man's call?
Is there no more love, in this world of hate?
Hearts made hard, love won't penetrate.
Seems the whole world, is suddenly without care,
A love that once was, is no longer there.

By Terry Webb

"EVER PRESENT LOVE"

As I meditate on You, "O" Lord"
I feel Thy presence near,
You always keep me sheltered in
Thy love for me so dear.
How wonderful Lord, to know that You
Are watching from above,
My heart is open to receive
Your ever present love.

By Terry Webb

"FIRST SEEK GOD"

We all seek pastures never touched
Or tampered by life's pain,
God will give us scorching heat
Before He sends the rain.

God wants us to acknowledge Him
And seek His will to do,
For if you seek, you soon will find
God gives all things to you.

Written By: Terry Webb

"FAITHFUL TO END"

God is my love in the Heavens-
His faithfulness reaches the skies,
His love and kindness to me I praise,
For every proof is in my eyes.

He is faithful in all His promises to man-
His Word is right and true,
Blessed is He whose help is God-
The Lord is faithful to you.

God is faithful, on all His promises-
His proof is unfailing love,
The maker of earth, and everything within-
The sea and the Heavens above.

I will not take my love from Him-
But only will I prevail,
Forever maintaining my love for Him-
My covenant will never fail

By Terry Webb

"SIMPLE TASK #1"

A simple task, to help you grow,
Show your love light, let it glow.
Fill your heart, with Heavens light,
You will grow, radiantly bright.

By Terry Webb

GIVE LOVE AWAY

Love in your heart, was not put there to stay,
Love is not love, till you give it away.
Real love is love, when you learn to give,
Jesus gave His life, that we should live.
There are many ways, to reach out with love,
Love is a gift, from God above.
Love is not love, till you give it away,
Love is not love, till you live it each day.
Love in your heart is there to stay,
Please share your love, with someone today.

By Terry Webb

"I GIVE YOU JESUS"

I give unto you, one true, devoted friend,
I give you Jesus, whose love will never end.
When you're feeling down, or ever in despair,
He will comfort you, with His love and care.

He will touch your heart, and your inner soul,
With a strong love that only he can control.
A kind friend He is; a strong friend indeed,
He's always by your side, whenever you're in need.

I give you Jesus, because His love is true,
I know His love, so I share His love with you.
There is no one else I know, that I could recommend,
That would truly devote Himself, to be such a friend.

There is nothing, for you, that Jesus will not do,
Within His great power, He even died for you.
So, turn yourself and hide, from sin to the cure,
For He has taken the wrath, to make your life pure.

Just as you are, Jesus will receive,
He'll welcome you with pardon; He'll cleanse and relieve.
That's why I give you Jesus, Christ the Lord above,
His life He gave for you, He did this out of love.

I give you Jesus, because His love is true,
There is no greater love, that I can give to you.
I give you Jesus, from whom all blessings flow,
His love is truly shown to all creatures here below.

I give unto you, a love that will never end,
I give you Jesus, a true devoted friend.
I give you Jesus, with no price to bring,
I give you Jesus, to His cross to cling!

By Terry Webb

"I AM"

I am the light unto this world-
To brighten up each day,
So turn your eyes on Me, my child-
To guide and lead thy way.

I am the bread of life, I am-
Also the true vine,
I am the way the truth, the life-
To all who would be mine.

I am the good Sheppard, I am-
Also Heavens door,
I am the resurrection of life;
Death reigns no more.

I am the Alpha and the Omega-
I drew salvations plan,
I am the breath of life to all-
I am the life to man.

I am the river of life, I am-
The light to all mankind;
I am the Lord, who reigns above-
Seek, and you shall find.

I am, the sacrifice for sin-
I am, that precious lamb,
I am, "Jesus Christ the Lord"
I am the great "I AM"

By Terry Webb

"THANK YOU LORD"

I give You thanks "O" Lord ", my God
For all you've done for me,
To You I give my thanks dear Lord
From sin you set me free.

"O" Lord," You have been merciful
You heard my inner cry,
I give my thanks to you alone
You did not pass me by.

By Terry Webb

TAKE COVER, CHILD

Take cover, child, and hide within Me,
For you live in dangerous territory.
Long ago, even before your birth,
I lived, and knew the pitfalls of earth.
The prince of this world even confronted Me,
Tempting Me with all of his treachery.
Take cover, child, for he is after you.
He will confront, and even tempt you, too.
Hide within Me, in the shadow of My wing,
From all the enemies the devil may bring.
Open your eyes unto his devious ways,
"Watch out!" He will trap you, if he may.
Stay close to Me, for I will protect,
Take cover, child, my child elect!

By Terry Webb

"THE ANGEL OF DEATH"

The angel of death, may come your way,
Any time of night, or any time of day.
He may come, at any given hour,
When he comes, death is his power.
You cannot hide, and you cannot run,
You can't escape death, Jesus was the only one.
When death comes, you'll surely know,
Death will hit you with his fatal blow.
When he hits, you will surely cry,
Prepare yourselves, we are all destined to die.
What can we do, what can be done?
Live for Jesus, God's only begotten Son.
Repent good people, we are all reprobate,
Turn your sins to rend, before it's to late!
Don't let death find you, unclean and unsaved,
Before death sends you to your fatal grave.
For it is written, that all men must die,
When death comes, you'll hear the cry.
Death always finds, a place to go,
Death's timing, you'll never know.
"But Jesus," He paid the cost!
He gave His life, for all were lost.
Live for Jesus, and you will be saved,
After death, He opens your grave.
Remember Death may come, night or day,
But the Angel of death, will come your way!

By Terry Webb

"STUBBORN CHILD"

"O" stubborn child of God take heed-
Let the Lord be thy guide,
To lead you from life's darkened maze-
And sin you try to hide.

When He gives you trials to face-
He helps you pass them through,
He shows you that His love and mercy-
Is at work in you.

So turn your eyes upon the Lord-
Look full upon His face,
See the goodness of His love-
His glory and His grace.

Come out, "O" stubborn child of God-
Change what's wrong in thee,
For God has sent His only Son-
To set all captives free.

He has a purpose in your life-
He wants you to pursue,
The calling that He gave to you-
His purpose, He said do!!!

By Terry Webb

"SHARE MY SORROW"

Comfort me my Lord, I pray-
Heal this heart of mine,
I put my trust in you alone-
Your love it is divine.

The only thing that I have to give-
Is brokenness and strife,
But please, except me as I am-
And beautify my life.

All that I ever had in life-
Is lost or gone away,
Restore to me new life, my Lord-
This to you, I pray.

Forever is your Word O Lord-
I surrender myself to Thee,
My life is in your hands dear Lord-
Let blessings fall on me.

Lead me to the living waters-
And be there by my side,
You know my soul is thirsty Lord-
Don't let me be denied.

You told me Lord that you'll be there-
For all of my tomorrow,
O Lord I pray that you would come-
And share with me my sorrow.

BY Terry Webb

"REAP THE HARVEST"

Go ye into all the lands
And spread my precious Word,
Go and tell the world of Me
For some has never heard.

The good you do is never lost
Some souls in me will root,
Everywhere you sow my Word
In time, will bear it's fruit.

You may not have the courage child
But mine I give to you,
For I, the Lord will strengthen you
My spirit will see you through.

Go, and reap the harvest now
Where others fear to tread,
And I will place a crown of gold
With jewels on thine head.

By Terry Webb

PRECIOUS LOVE

Love is amazingly precious,
And worth the price of loss.
Love is beautiful to know,
That Christ has paid it's cost,
It was love that paid the price,
Christ, the Lord did give.
He gave His life through precious love,
In Him we all now live!

By Terry Webb

"LEAD ME TO HEAVEN"

Lead the way for me to follow-
To your world of peace and love,
Keep me on the righteous path-
To Your kingdom up above.

Once I'm there I know I'll find-
Much joy new love and care,
A new life for me and comfort-
These things await me there.

Please lead me to this Heaven-
My Jesus, I pray to Thee,
Guide my steps along the way-
And please watch over me.

Please lead me to this Heaven-
My Lord, to you I pray,
Take me to the stairway-
So I may start this day.

Written by: Terry Webb

"HIS LOVE FOREVER"

His love is forever, it has no end,
His love has conquered, over all sin.
No matter if you're black, white, or brown,
You will see that his love, is always around.

It does not matter, what color you are,
He loves you still, and never too far.
Through His love, He died for you,
He did this for, the sin you do.

His love is wonderful, it is forever,
He will never change, no not ever.
He is the Beginning, and also the End,
Our LORD JESUS, HAS CONQUERED SIN!

Written by: Terry Webb

"HE IS CALLING YOUR NAME"

"Shhh Listen," can you hear it-
Do you hear the voice?
He's calling out your name-
You're His special choice.
This is nothing strange-
Nor is it fantasy,
He's calling out your name,
He's also calling me.
You are never too unspiritual-
To be a chosen one,
God will make you whole-
As you share life with His Son.
He is calling out your name-
With a still small voice,
"Shhh Listen," Can you hear it?
You're His special choice.

By: TERRY WEBB

"HE IS!"

He is the Alpha and the Omega
The beginning and the end,
He is the one whom created all
He created all men.
He is the mighty wind that blows
That calm a raging sea,
He is the helper to all mankind
He even comforts thee.
He is the sun which gives us light
He is the cedars tall,
He is the rocky mountains high
Also the waterfall.
He is the hand that reaches out
His is the only one,
For He is "Jesus," creator of all
In truth, He is "God's Son."
Come to Him and now be saved
Come children of man,
For who can stand against Him?
There is no one that can!

By Terry Webb

"HE HAS PROMISED"

God has given a promise-
For all our every needs,
His promises has been planted-
In all of mankind's seed.

Never will He leave you-
Never will He forsake you,
Never has He failed you-
Although people do.

God's word support thee-
His promises sustain thee,
His promises have not failed thee-
He keeps His word to thee.

I've failed to keep a promise-
Others have failed me too,
But God will keep a promise-
He make's to me and you.

The Lord is Thy Sheppard-
He's with you always,
From the beginning of all time-
And till the end of all day's . . .

By: TERRY WEBB

"GRACE IS FOUND"

Why must you keep on hurting Me
Why persecute thou Me?
Why do you choose to place Me back
Upon that dreadful tree?

How many times will you crucify
And scorn My Holy Name?
How many times will you openly
Put My Name to shame?

How many times must I forgive
Thy ravages of sin?
When will you open up your heart
To let Me dwell within?

When will you trust in Me my child
To guide and lead thy **soul?**
When will you give your life to Me
That I may have control?

Behold, consider what I've done
I left my throne above,
To shed My blood and purge your sins
I did this out of love.

So why must you continue child
In sin that has you bound?
My truth and love is clearly shown
Through me, grace is found!

By Terry Webb

"GOD THE CREATOR!"

What may be known of God is shown-
His greatness is surely seen,
The master designer of the Heaven's-
The sea and forest green.

All of creation points to Him-
All creatures great and small,
In the image of Him He made mankind-
God, He made us all.

By Terry Webb

"JESUS" YOU TOLD ME

You told me things, that I must do,
To walk straight in the eyes of You.
You told me start out with a prayer,
Addressed to Gods, love and care.
You told me yesterdays troubles and sorrow,
Will be lifted with a better tomorrow.
You told me that I must believe,
All Your promises in order to receive.
You told me "stand tall," don't be afraid,
That all things in this day, You have made.
You told me that in all things I do,
To keep my mind and heart on You.
You told me to trust Your love and care,
I thank you Lord, for being there.

Written by: Terry Webb

"NEVER A TEARDROP"

The hand of God is always there
To Guard His children well,
Nothing is hid from the eyes of God
His saints, securely dwell.
Never a teardrop, within their hearts
His saints shall never see,
Within this life, or the life to come
All tears of pain shall flee.

By Terry Webb

"MY LIFE TO JESUS"

I give my life, and all my love
To Jesus who died for me,
His precious blood fell to the ground
At a place called Calvary.

I hold my hands out to the heavens
My heart for Him to receive,
The love He gave upon the cross
He still lives, and I believe.

For the life He gave upon the cross
High on Calvary,
Has saved my soul from Satan's hold
And made me whole and free.

So I give my heart to Jesus Christ
For all that He has done,
He gave His life for all to live
From sin, The battle is won!

Written by: Terry Webb

"WHO AM I"

I am the Alpha and the Omega-
The beginning and the end,
I am the resurrection of life-
I am the light to men.

I am the bread of life to man-
I am the living bread,
I also am the Word of life-
Through Me all men are fed.

I am the life, the truth, the way-
The Glory of the sun,
I am the Lord, Jesus Christ-
In truth, I am Gods Son.

Written by: Terry Webb

"WALK WITH GOD"

Let us learn to walk with God-
And shed all earthly care,
He will guide and lead the way
His love, He will share.

Although the journey may be long-
And we at times are weak,
The Lord will give the strength we need-
By word, He will speak.

His words are life, our daily bread-
We need Him everyday,
Walk with Him and talk with Him-
For strength along the way.

By: TERRY WEBB

YOU ARE MY STRENGTH "EACH DAY"

It is God who gives us strength-
To make our perfect way,
It is God who takes hold-
And strengthens us each day.

It is God who is the strength-
To people young and old,
It is God who is the strength
That turns the meek heart bold.

It is God who gives us strength-
Where It cannot be found,
It is God who is the strength-
To everyone around.

It is God who is my strength-
Through life's journey way,
It is God who is my strength-
He is my strength each day!

By: TERRY WEBB

"O" LUCIFER

Oh how you have fallen "O" Lucifer
Morning star, son of the dawn,
You have lifted thyself above Thy God
Thy sins had just begun.

You said in your heart you will raise your throne
Above the stars of God,
You said you will sit on the mount of assembly
But yet, you were brought to sod!

You said you will rise above the clouds
Like God, the most high,
You have made your self to be a god
For this you now must die.

Like a falling star from Heaven you fell
Satan has became your name,
You lied and called yourself a god
But God didn't play your game.

"O" Lucifer, O how you have fallen
Satan, you are now a snake,
One day you will burn for eternity
With fire made of a lake.

By Terry Webb

"A GREAT LOVE"

There is a love that holds together
Forever always true,
This love is Jesus Christ the Lord
Who gave His life for you.

He proved it on that dreadful cross
The pain He did endure,
There is no greater love than His
With Him love is secure.

By Terry Webb

"MY HEART'S DESIRE"

My hearts desire, is to know the Lord
To change my heart within,
Your power Lord, is eternal life
And power over sin.
My hearts desire is to know your grace
You're my life, and my way,
To know Your love, is what I want
To walk with You each day.

By Terry Webb

"I'LL BE WITH YOU"

My promise is this, to you my child-
I never will leave you alone,
I will never leave or forsake you-
My child, you are my own.

So when you grow weak in your struggles-
Midst the storms and thunders that roll,
My child, my strength will be with you-
To bring peace unto thy soul.

By: TERRY WEBB

HIS GREAT SURPRISE

Each day the sun rises to the skies,
The Lord, our God, has a great surprise.
Though' first He shines the light of day,
He helps guide man along the way.
Side by side with man He walks,
Inside man's ear, He also talks
Directing man with His still voice,
An awesome God, let man rejoice.
The beauty of all, life around,
A great surprise, where love abounds.
The magnificent trees, and beautiful flowers,
Are the work of God, even rainy showers.
Behold the beauty to man's mere eyes,
They're all God's wonders, HIS GREAT SURPRISE!

By Terry Webb

"ACCEPT CHRIST NOW"

Now is the appointed time my friend-
Accept Christ while you can,
The promise of God is not tomorrow-
Tomorrow is uncertain,
He who believes is not condemned-
Accept Christ while you may,
For tomorrow isn't promised to man-
God's promise is today.

By: TERRY WEBB

"CLEANSE ME LORD"

Help me be to You, Oh Lord
Clean and pure within,
Cleanse me with your precious blood
Please take all thought of sin.

I come to your most Holy Throne
And at Thy feet I bow,
I know "O" Lord, that by your word
That You will help me now.

By Terry Webb

GROW TO KNOW JESUS

Growing to know Jesus, becomes increasing delight,
A glorious life to anticipate, living in His light.
No longer an obligation, to a lifeless discipline,
Changed from his day; all activities with men.
Ultimately changed in life, because the time is near,
Longing for His glorious return, when Jesus reappears.

By Terry Webb

"HIS LIFE FOR OURS"

He died for the sins of the world-
He was raised for our justification,
His blood was shed one time for all-
The sins of every nation!

His empty sepulcher has to say-
This to both you and me,
It tell us that He died and rose-
To set His people free.

By Terry Webb

"WISDOM"

A man's wisdom makes his face to shine
But where does wisdom come,
The Lord he gives wisdom and knowledge
Even more He gives to some.

He grants to all mankind a measure
Of wisdom, holy and true,
To love God is the beginning of wisdom
Acknowledging all you do.

By Terry Webb

"ALL PRAISE THE KING"

Let us adore and give Him praise
For His power and His might,
May we never lose the sight of Him
And give to Him, His right.
For as the Angels praise His name
In Heaven high above,
Like them our praise should never cease
Praise the King of love.

By Terry Webb

BE NOT DISMAYED

Let not your heart be troubled,
Nor let it be dismayed;
I came to give you peace, my child,
I heard you when you prayed.
You believe in God, do you?
Believe also in Me;
I am the way, the truth, the life;
I've come to set you free!

By Terry Webb

"CHRIST PAID"

Because the Lord has paid the price
Salvation now is free,
All our sins on Him were laid
When He died upon that tree.

Therefore, our debt is fully paid
By His life's sacrifice,
We now are saved from wrath through Him
The Lord he paid the price.

Written By: Terry Webb

FOREVER THE SAME

God is the same today, tomorrow
Always, and forever,
He is the same for eternity
Never changing never.

His mighty word endures forever
His law is fixed on high,
His faithfulness unto all men
Abided forever nigh.

So turn your eye's upon Him now
And call upon His name,
He is the beginning and the end
Forever He's the same.

By Terry Webb

"THE RISEN LORD"

We must look beyond the empty tomb
And the cross at Calvary
Then we will see a risen Lord
With life eternally

He died and rose again one day
How strange, yet wholly true
Now His nailed scarred hands extends
Life, for me and you

By Terry Webb

"BE NOT AFRAID"

God is there always, protecting thee
His child you'll always be,
When fear knocks, trust Him completely
The fear you have will flee.
Abhor what is evil, cling to what's good
Prove the devil a lie,
Lift up the lamp of God, my friend
Be not afraid to die.

By Terry Webb

"I SHALL WAIT"

Truly my soul waits upon my Lord-
From Him comes my salvation,
I seek Thee Lord, your Grace and power-
Also your Holy nation.
I shall not be moved, my soul thirsts-
I shall do valiantly,
And my Lord will quench, my thirsty soul-
With life eternally.

By Terry Webb

"AWESOME GOD"

We serve an awesome God
His power we can't deny,
We see His power in lighting storms
His thunder shakes the sky.

He holds the entire universe
By just His word alone,
The earth He made His footstool
And Heaven is His throne.

Written by: Terry Webb

"BEHOLD, YOUR KING"

One day the King of Kings will come
And reign upon this earth,
As sure as the prophets said He'll come
Before His earthly birth.

On that day the earth will shake-
The Heavenly Hosts shall sing,
Behold, thy King has come to you-
Thy Lord and Sovereign King,

His chosen then will come to Him-
His elect, He will embrace,
All things of earth will bow to Him-
For the glory of His grace.

Behold, the King of Kings will come
Bright as the morning star,
Behold, our King is coming for us,
His light we'll see afar.

By Terry Webb

"CHANGED WITHIN"

Teach me Lord, what I must do,
In order to live my life with You.
Open my eyes, so I may see,
The path of life, You lead for me.
Do not despise, my sinning soul,
Have mercy Lord, please make me whole.
I know my life is all but true,
But Lord, my soul shall boast in You.

By Terry Webb

"DOING GODS WILL"

It matters not what others do
Nor what they even say,
When we choose to serve the Lord
Or when we choose to pray.

We are the light unto this world
In ridicule and fun,
For when the Lord comes for His own
He'll say to us, "Well Done."

Written by: Terry Webb

"EVERY IDLE WORD"

The tongue is a weapon, this is very true,
And this deadly weapon, lives inside of you.
The tongue is a messenger, from the human heart,
That speak good or evil, it can tear things apart.
Man will be accounted, for every idle word,
All words ever spoken, all words ever heard.
Evil words are deadly, they can deceive or even bruise,
So be very careful, my friend, in the words you choose.
Cause some words are poison, they hurt, and even kill,
So think before you speak, don't speak as you feel.

By Terry Webb

FOLLOW ME

Take up thy cross, and follow Me,
Nor think of death, but life you'll see.
Whoever saves, his life will lose,
The choice is yours. you now must choose.
For only he, who bears his cross,
New life he'll find, and not be lost.

By Terry Webb

FATHER IN HEAVEN

Father in Heaven, I pray to Thee,
Protect and watch, over me.
Guide and lead, me every day,
Please let me not, go astray.
Father in Heaven, the most high,
Comfort me, for when I cry.
I'm like a sheep, upon Your land,
Keep me in, Your loving hand.
Father in Heaven, God of the living,
Thank You Lord, for generously giving.
This life to me, and all things there of,
But thank You mostly, for Your Precious Love!

By Terry Webb

"SIMPLE TASK 2"

A simple task, to do today,
Praise the Lord, in a special way . . .

By Terry Webb

GOD IS

The God of might,
The God of light,
The God who made,
The sunshine bright.
The God of Truth,
Also of love,
The God who made,
The Heavens above.
He is the keeper,
Of every soul,
The only God,
That can make one whole.
The God of Peace,
God is forgiving,
God is God,
Of all the living!

By Terry Webb

"I AM WITH YOU"

Let not your heart be troubled
Nor let if be dismayed,
For I am with you always, child
Do not be afraid.

Yes, I was there with you
Upon your day of birth,
And I will even be with you
Through all your days on earth.

For when you pass through trials of fire
or even oceans deep,
I, the Lord will be with you
Thy soul I will keep.

Written By: Terry Webb

"TEACH YOUR CHILD"

Teach your child, in the ways of God
And they will never stray,
Teach them how to trust in Him
To worship Him and pray.

Teach them all, to know their God
To render Him control,
Teach them, they must give to Him
Their mind, heart, and soul.

By Terry Webb

SURPRISE WITHIN MY EYES

One day in wonder, I closed my eyes,
I saw within, a great surprise.
I saw a love that filled the air,
I saw joy, with Jesus there.
Face to face, He talked with me,
Side by side, we were walking, free.
He told me things that won my heart,
That His love for me, would not depart.
He promised me a place, in Heaven above,
Signed His promise, with His own love.
Now each day, I look towards the skies,
That same surprise, is within my eyes.

By Terry Webb

"REFLECTIONS"

Oh Lord, please help us live our lives
That people will then see,
Reflections of Your caring heart
Your love and purity.

Please help us love what's good and right
And make us pure within,
Please teach us Lord to love the truth
And lose all sense of sin.

By Terry Webb

PRAYER OF PROTECTION

I rise before the morning sun
To seek Thy Holy Throne,
To declare your loving—kindness, Lord,
And pray to you alone.
My trust is placed in you alone
My shield from desolation,
That's why I kneel before your Throne,
"O" God of my salvation.
Protect me from the evil one
Please keep me from alarm,
I pray for your right hand, dear Lord,
To keep me from all harm.
Uphold me, Lord, I pray to Thee
I pray to Thee alone,
I call upon your Holy name,
"O" Lord, I am thine own!

By Terry Webb

LIVING WATER

Only Jesus, the Living Water
Can quench our thirsty soul,
Only Jesus, the Living Water
Can cleanse and make one whole.
"If anyone should thirst for life-
Let him come to me,
Thine heart will flow Living Waters
Of life eternally."
Give to me this Living Water,
"O" Lord, will you bestow?
That life-giving Living Water,
Unto your child below.

By Terry Webb

"HIS STAR"

Learn to shine brightly, on your bending knees-
God who see's your heart, is the only one to please,
You are His precious star, that Jesus sets aglow-
To show His loving kindness, to all who seek to know,
You are His precious star, cause Jesus shines within-
A super star, His star, reflecting light to men.

By: TERRY WEBB

"HE IS SO WONDERFUL"

The door to his heart, is always unlatched,
His love come not, with strings attached.
No one can match, His generosity,
No one can do, anything as He.
Our lives is shared, with His love each day,
He is light to shadows, that fall our way.
He make life worthwhile, and peaceful to me,
He is so wonderful, as wonderful can be.

Written by: Terry Webb

"HE IS NEVER TO BUSY"

He is never to busy, to help when you fall,
He is never to busy, to answer a prayer call.
He is never to busy, to hear the songs you sing,
He is never to busy, although He's Lord and King.
He is never to busy, to wipe the tears from your eye,
He is never to busy, to comfort when you cry.
He is never to busy, to take away the pain,
He is never to busy, to bring or stop the rain.
He is never to busy, to help when He can,
He is never to busy, to help His creation "MAN!"

Written by: Terry Webb

GOD WILL SUPPLY

Fret not my child of earthly things
They'll never satisfy,
The inner soul within thy self
That I, The Lord supply.
I will supply Thy every need
Thy trust put forth in Me,
The secret to a full filled life
Let Me supply for thee . . .

By Terry Webb

"JESUS AND ME"

Jesus is my light, He is my whole life,
He is closer to me, than even my wife.
He's closer than my children, even all my friends,
Because he is always with me, in times I think its the end.

He is my friend and my playmate, none better can be found,
Because He is with me, when nobody else is around.
To break it all down, He is everything to be,
That's why in my life. It's Jesus and me.

Written by: Terry Webb

"NO NEED FOR LIGHT"

There will be a Holy city
Out of heaven it will descend,
And in this Glorious city
Will live chosen righteous men.

The gates will never be shut
And much glory it shall bring,
For nothing shall enter in
To cause abomination or anything.

This city will be great
It will have no need for light,
The glory of God will illuminate it
And the Lamb will be it's Light.

Written by: Terry Webb

"MY EVERYTHING"

Everything and more, God he is to me,
My Lord, My God, He has set me free.
He is the light, unto my eye,
He is my comfort, when I cry.
He is my joy, for when I'm sad;
He is my happiness, He makes me glad.
He is my life, everything there of-
But most of all, He is my love.

By Terry Webb

"WHO IS HE?"

Who is He, who made the earth?
Who is He, who gave it worth?
Who is He, made appear the dry land?
Who is He, who created a living man?
Who is He, who called the sun to give light?
Who is He, who separated day from night?
Who is He, who makes the rain?
Who is He, who endured life's pain?
Who is He, who made each and every star?
Who made the flowers, beautiful as they are?
Who made the ocean's, and sky so blue?
Who made the trees, and animals too?
Who made cold, the flakes of snow?
Who made the storms, and cold wind blow?
Who made each man, to live eternally?
He is so wonderful, "GOD IS HE!"

By Terry Webb

"WHAT JESUS REALLY WANTS"

What Jesus really wants
Give Him priority,
Christ deserves our hearts
Free and willingly.

What He really wants
For man to obey,
Self-denial discipleship
Requires that we pray.

What he really wants
Is love kind and true,
Jesus calls our hearts
He also tests us too.

"O Lord by your mercies
May we hear Thy call,
Jesus really wants us
To love Him most of all.

By Terry Webb

"YOU GIVE"

You give me light, that I may see,
You give the birds, a resting tree.
You give children, a care free life,
You give some men, a loving wife.
You give me rest, unto my bed,
You give me food, so I am fed.
You give overall, to me Your love,
You give abundantly from Heaven above.

By Terry Webb

"O" PRECIOUS LAMB

Worthy is the Lamb of God
Whom died at the cross,
The Lamb, whom died is He who lives
For those who now are lost.
Every knee shall bow to Him
To Him for sinners slain,
Honor and glory and also blessing
Forever the Lamb to reign.
Oh how precious is this Lamb
Worthy is His name,
Lord of my life, Jesus Christ
Christ, my spirit claim.

By Terry Webb

"BUT ONCE"

In this world we live but once
Not passing this way again,
We are responsible for every act
Of good works, even sin.

No matter who we are in life
We must watch the things we do,
To not indulge in sinful lusts
Cause God is watching you.

For every act of sin we do
Surely, we will pay,
Whether we pay right here on earth
Or there on judgment day.

So remember my friends, we live but once
Be careful not to be had,
We will be judged, on judgment day
By works, good and bad . . .

By Terry Webb

I'M JESUS "REMEMBER ME"

You were lost, then I came, now you are found,
You were on the road of destruction,
Truly death for you was bound.
You followed me and listened, to the words I had to say,
But somehow you became lost again, on your journey way.
I didn't want you lost in this open world of sin,
So I got on your trail and found you, I picked you up again.
I didn't want you forever lost, so I laid down my life for you,
I felt the sorrow and the pain, this life was putting you thru.
So remember Me, remember the cross,
When ever you get lost,
Remember I died to save you from sin, My life was the cost!

Written by: Terry Webb

"HALLOWED BE HIS NAME"

Swear not at all, for the scriptures forbid,
All words you speak, from God are not hid.
We have no right, to misuse Gods name,
Even some Christians, are not without blame.

Hallowed be His name, speak not in vain,
Don't dishonor God, in words of profane.
Let us not condone, but let's make sure,
The words we use, with God are pure.

Written by: Terry Webb

"A WISHFUL PRAYER"

I asked for strength, that I might achieve-
To accomplish the things, that I believe,
God made me weak, that I might obey-
To do the things, in which He say.
I asked for health, that I might do greater-
In my life, a little later,
I was given grace, that I might do good-
If I obey the Lord, as I truly should.
I asked for riches, that I might live high-
Like a king, up in the sky,
I was given poverty, that I might be wise-
And know the Lord, in Heaven's skies.
I asked for power, that I might have the praise of men-
And overcome, this world within,
I was given weakness, that I might feel the need of God-
On every road, to which I trod.
I asked for all things, that I might enjoy life-
And to overcome, life's bitter strife,
I was given life, that I might enjoy all things-
While praising the Lord, in everything.
I received nothing, I asked for, even hoped for,
But my prayers were answered, forever more.

By: TERRY WEBB

"CLOCK OF LIFE"

Our life is measured by the second
Minute and the hour,
No one knows when time will stop
Only God has this power.

The clock of life is wound but once
And it will stop one day,
The life we live is but a test
To serve God and obey.

So we must keep in step with God
To live a life that's true,
keep in mind the clock of life
In everything you do.

One day the silver cord will break
Then time will close it's door,
The clock of life will stop my friend
And life will be no more.

So do not waste your time in sin
For time will end one day,
Though God provides the grace to win
We must serve Him and obey.

By Terry Webb

TRIALS

Each trial you face there's reason
Someday the light you'll see,
God only ask you trust in Him
Thy side He's there with thee.
His purpose is to mold your life
From darkness into light,
To walk the path of life with Him
By faith and not by sight.

By Terry Webb

"SINS REMEDY"

This world is filled with so much hate
Torn from God with sin,
Why is this world the way it is
The answer is found within.

The heart of man is filled with evil
Hate, also with greed,
This problem occurred in the day's of Adam
God's word he took no heed.

He disobeyed the Heavenly Father
God's word, true and sweet,
He disobeyed when he ate of the fruit
The fruit, God said don't eat.

Sin entered in the heart of man
Right then without delay,
That's why the world became corrupt
And sinful till this day.

God, He gave His only Son
A sacrifice for our sin,
For the wages of sin, is only death
He died in place of men.

He gladly suffered upon the cross
He died in our place,
He took our sins, and He bore
Our shame and our disgrace.

Those who look to faith in Him
Eternal life shall gain,
Those who don't believe He's Lord
Their sins with them remain!

By Terry Webb

"WITH HIS HANDS"

With His hands I receive strength
For work He bids me do,
With His hands I am made strong
His hands do pull me through.

With His hands I'm made secure
Protected from alarm,
His hands will always comfort me
And keep me from all harm.

With His hand in hand with mine
I shall not be afraid,
His hands of love will lead me through
Death's dark veil of shade.

By Terry Webb

ALL IS GOD'S

Magical, mystical wonders of God
Is what our eyes do see,
For since the beginning of all creation
God will always be.
The wind, the water, the light and sod
His goodness He displays,
All of creation do point to God
And all do give Him Praise!

By Terry Webb

"CHRIST PAID THE PRICE"

Oh the grace that set me free
Through faith I'm justified,
I've been redeemed and all because
For me, my Savior died.

My Savior's nail scarred hands extend
Forgiveness for my sin,
His blood ran down to cleanse my heart
To make me whole within.

To think of His great sacrifice
Upon that dreadful tree,
That tree in which they made a cross
And placed on Calvary.

My Savior gave His life on it
Before all sight of Heaven,
Through Him I now am truly blessed
My sins are now forgiven.

Christ, He paid sins price for me
My sins on Him were laid,
I've been redeemed, I'm justified
The price of sin is paid.

By Terry Webb

"DEVOTION"

Upon my life shed forth Thy grace
Although I strayed from Thee
Beholding the glory of the cross
Thou gave Thy life for me

I am resolved, no longer to linger
Make Thy name my trust
To keep in step with You O Lord
And dwell amongst the just

By Terry Webb

FOREVER TRUE

Always and forever, forever true,
The Lord will always be with you.
Beside your side, along the way,
Your help in need throughout the day.
A friend to you He is indeed.
He will always help, when you're in need.
He gives His gentle touch of grace,
He shines His love upon your face.
His heart is love; you can't compare,
A love like His-To always care.
Unconditional love He gives to you,
A wonderful love, FOREVER TRUE!

By Terry Webb

"I SURRENDER"

Forever is thy Word, O Lord-
I surrender myself to Thee,
My times are in your hand O Lord-
Let thy blessings fall on me.

Fill me with thy love and power-
Thy Word I will profess,
To prove thy doctrine all divine-
My lips they will express.

By Terry Webb

THIS TELLS ME

With the rising sun in each new day,
Tells me something, in which that say.
The Lord, My God, is up above,
To guide my way with His true love.
To bend my way in righteousness,
Through darkness in a world as this.
The sun above shows He is there,
The warm feeling tells me He cares.

By Terry Webb

"ALWAYS"

In the Lords hands, I am always,
Till the end of time, ending all days.
My spirit rests, under His protecting wing,
My soul is comforted, even my heart sing.

From the joy and love, every day that I live,
Blessed be the Lord, to me that give.
Always faithful, and always forgiving,
Always merciful, to all the living.
.
He's always giving, love abundantly,
Always loving, both you and me.
Wait on the Lord, and keep His way's,
And He will exalt you, in life always.

Written by: Terry Webb

"BEAUTY IN YOU"

The spirit of God dwell's in our hearts
Showing through us his love,
Could you be called a beautiful Christian?
Yes, with God above.

By Terry Webb

"CHILD OF GOD"

A child of God is always welcome
His pardon awaits for you,
If you are His, but turned away
From what you know is true.

He urges you to come back home
To serve Him faithfully,
He has a home prepared for you
With Him Eternally.

So, turn aside from evil things
To God your sins confess,
Then live your life unto the Lord
In Christian Holiness.

By Terry Webb

"DON'T GIVE UP"

Don't give up, give God your all-
Give to Him, your all "n" all,
Don't give up, do not decline-
Continue across the finish line.
Don't give up, Jesus won the fight-
Darkness has been turned to light.

By: TERRY WEBB

"EVERYONE DREAMS"

Everyone has a dream in life-
To make it reality,
Let Jesus come into your heart-
Put all your faith in Thee.

Dreams are something God gives you-
That never fades away,
Success is built upon all dreams-
Influencing people today.

There is nothing wrong with dreaming-
In our lifetime through and through,
Precious dreams become reality-
With efforts applied by you.

Let your dreams have it's perfect work-
Let God refine it like gold,
For in God's time He'll show you why-
Then blessing greatly unfold.
DREAMS DO COME TRUE!

Written By: Terry Webb

"FOLLOW THE STAR"

I am the bright and morning star-
Come and follow Me,
I will lead you to a better life-
Life Eternally.

I will guide and lead the way for you-
Come now and receive,
I offer eternal life for all-
But, you must believe.

You must believe, I am the truth-
The life, and the way,
Your faith and trust must be in Me-
My Words you must obey.

I will lead your soul to it's new life-
Through all Eternity,
I am the bright and morning star-
Come and follow Me.

By Terry Webb

"FEAR NOT"

In the valley of the shadow of death
Where darkness seeks thine soul,
Blessed hope through our Lord Jesus
Life, eternal our goal.

For our lives our Saviors blood was shed
Now we have obtained grace,
And when aligned, with God's true Word
We need not fear death's place.

By Terry Webb

"SIMPLE TASK 3"

A simple little task, that you can do
Forgive someone, God forgave you.

By Terry Webb

"GOD"

All things are in my hands my child
You have nothing to fear,
For I am with you always child
I, the Lord am near.

So, take time out to be with me
I will encourage you,
Give you strength for tasks ahead
This, my child I'll do.

I also will provide for you
So in all things you'll grow,
Also, I'll give to you my mind
With it my child you'll know.

My promise lies ahead for you
With Me my child you'll trod,
Continue with my works dear one
And know that **I Am God!**

Written By: TERRY WEBB

"I NEED THE LORD"

Oh how I need, the Lord my God
On each road, in which I trod,
I need Him in my walk of life
I need Him for my bitter strife.

I need the Lord, to guide my way
To guide my footsteps, through each day,
In my battles, His shield and sword
Protect me always, I need You Lord.

Written by: Terry Webb

THE BIBLE

The Bible is God's **B**asic **I**nstruction
Before **L**eaving **E**arth,
The Bible is the Word of God
A map to spirit birth.

The Bible is our daily food
To gain strength and light,
The Bible is the wisdom of God
To guide our steps upright.

The Bible is God's Word of life
Alive through all the ages,
The Bible is the key to life
With wisdom in it's pages.

The Bible is God's mighty Word
To guard His children well,
The Bible is a path to life
Where saints securely dwell.

By Terry Webb

"SURRENDER TO HIS LOVE"

Take a look at God's love, then you'll surrender-
To find fulfillment, in a love that's tender,
Look deep into His love, find what it mean-
To live in a love, so pure and clean,
Surrender your heart, unto His love-
His divine gift, from Heaven above.

By: TERRY WEBB

"RIVER OF LIFE"

From this river, I give to thee-
Life for you, eternally.
This river flows, only from my throne-
This drink I give, only to my own.
Draw not away, come unto me;
I am that river of life to thee.
Drink my child, and you will live-
Eternal life, to you I give.
Life for you, eternally-
From my river, I give unto thee.

By Terry Webb

"LIFE AFTER DEATH"

What will happen to a man
Upon his last of breath?
What will happen to his soul
At the time of death?

What will happen when his soul
leaves time and space?
Will there be another life
Or another dwelling place?

If there be another life
Where will this life be?
Where will our souls go to live
For all eternity?

Some people say, maybe Heaven
Or maybe even hell,
But, who's to say where souls will go
Only God can tell.

Our souls belong to God alone
Even our destiny,
There is a life, after death
A life of eternity.

God holds the key's of life and death
Of Heaven and of Hell,
But where our souls will go to live
Only God can tell!

By: TERRY WEBB

"HEAVENLY WISDOM"

A wise man endured with knowledge
Let him sow out good,
He should be sown in righteousness
That he truly should.
Only merciful good fruits and peace
And grace submit out love,
But bitter envying strife in your heart
descend not from above.
That wisdom is earthly, sensually devilish
against the truth that's pure,
There is great confusion in all evil works
The Lord cannot endure.
But the wisdom from above is pure
Peaceable without partiality,
The fruit of righteousness sown in peace
Make peace without hypocrisy.
Make peace works with meekness of wisdom
Be not bitter in strife,
Sown out of a good conversation
Be peacefully true in life.

Written by: Terry Webb

"HE IS WORTHY"

Worthy is the Lamb of God
For honor and for praise,
He is worthy of all praise of men
All their earthly days.
Even the Angels praise His name
For them it's true and right,
All mankind must do the same
With all their heart and might.

Written By: Terry Webb

"GOD'S UNCONDITIONAL LOVE"

A great love flows from the heart of God
His love divine, His love excelling,
He laid all our sins on His only Son
To fit us in His humble dwelling.

The joy of Heaven, to earth had come down
God's unflinching love from above,
Don't let a day go without thanking Him
For his unconditional love.

Written By: Terry Webb

"JESUS IS HE"

The maker of the Heavens
Creator of the earth,
Creator of the universe
The Author of birth.

The Alpha and Omega
The giver of all life,
The beginning and the end
Jesus, The Christ.

The morning star of glory
Forever to be,
The maker of all things
Jesus, Is He.

Written By: Terry Webb

NO NEED TO HIDE

Your life is sealed with Christ in God,
While on this planet, each road you trod.
He protects you from the terror talk,
And helps you in this pilgrimage walk.
There is no need for you to hide,
Christ, the Lord, is by your side.
No need to hide from earthly eyes,
Earthly eyes that will despise.
But set your mind on things above,
And also set your heart with love.
Combine them all, and you will find,
Unspeakable joy and peace of mind.
Dark shadows, and fears of old,
Cannot exist for the one who's bold.
There is no need for you to hide,
Let Christ be your strength and guide.

By Terry Webb

MY PERFECT LOVE

My perfect love, my wholeness lies
To God above, high in the skies,
How grateful I, whose help for me
Gave me life, and set me free.

I put my trust, and hope in God
And my feet, in peace are shod,
I have been bought, "YES "with a price
By the Lord, called Jesus Christ.

I've found a friend, He chose me
To be with Him, through eternity,
My perfect love, died in my place
I long to see, His loving face.

Written By: Terry Webb

"WHERE IS YOUR TREASURE"

Where your treasure is, your heart will be also,
So think my friend, where will your eternal life go.

Eternal life, is more valuable than gold,
More than all the diamonds, that were ever sold.

All the riches, of this entire living earth,
Cannot compare, to what eternal life is worth.

Remember that money, is the root to all evil,
You love money, then you serve the devil.

Money or God, who will you serve?
You chose money, you'll get what you deserve.

The devil is money, his heart is hate,
Give yourself to Jesus, before it's too late.

Forever will we live, in the presence of God,
We must prove ourselves, in this world we trod.

Surely all things will eventually pass away,
But the Word of God, is here to stay.

Remember nothing can compare, to life eternally,
In the presence of Jesus, "Lord and Majesty."

By Terry Webb

"YOU NEED JESUS"

Why do you always struggle so?
Christ died to set you free,
You cannot fight this fight alone
The Lord is there for thee.

The Lord Jesus Christ my friend
Will help along the way,
You need His hand of love my friend
trust in Him and pray.

By Terry Webb

"ON BENDED KNEE"

Let us bow to Him in worship, lets kneel before our creator,
Giving thanks and praise to Jesus, our loving mediator.
Let us put our hands together, and get on bending knee,
Thanking God almighty, for His son who set us free.

Let us pray to our maker, God in heaven above,
Through Jesus Christ our Savior, Lord of life and love.
Let us open up our hearts, Christ did for you and me,
Let us bow to Him in prayer, on our bending knee.

Written by: Terry Webb

"CONFESS YOUR SINS"

Your sins you cannot hide from God
For deep within your heart,
He knows the very thoughts that come
Before they even start.

If we confess our sins to Him
Our sins He will forgive,
Confession is the quickest way
Confess your sins and live.

Written by: Terry Webb

"IN HARMONY WITH GOD"

It's funny, how all things just fall in place,
All things that surrounds, the human race.
Even the rain, that falls from the Heavens above,
Is in harmony, with God's true love.
The breath of life, from the cool winds breeze-
Gives life to all, even plants and trees.
For one life to survive, it takes another to give,
It's life in exchange, so the new life may live.
Life is a cycle, that no one understands,
But everything is in harmony, within God's plan.

By Terry Webb

"GRATITUDE"

Thank You Lord, for blessing me
And giving me this day,
Thank You for Your guiding hand
For showing me the way.
May I, for these be grateful
For this You've done for me,
And I will always praise Your name
Through all Eternity.

By Terry Webb

"A PURE HEART"

Nothing can surpass the heart
Of one that's pure within,
They humbly bow their knees to God
To take all thought of sin.

They do their simple deeds of kindness
Though it's end, they may not see,
But God will bless them in their walk
Through all eternity.

By Terry Webb

"COME HOME"

Just as you are, come home my child-
I will welcome you from afar,
For I have come that you be saved-
Come child as you are.

Repent and give your life to me-
To gain new strength and light,
With me you'll find my precepts true-
To guide your steps upright.

By Terry Webb

"GODS WORD"

The Word of God is now my light
To help me see my way,
I read to know what He has said
To not be led astray.

I'll trust in His unchanging Word
To lead my pathway straight,
His Word shall guide and lead my soul
To Heavens open gate.

By Terry Webb

THE HEAVENS GLORY OF GOD

Enveloped in beauty, the silence of night,
Sprinkled with stars, in heaven bright.
In cloudless skies, the shimmering,
The heavenly stars, are rendering.
The glory of God, crisp and clear,
His wondrous glory, far, but near.
The heavenly show, of stars reveal,
God's magnificent glory, alive, and real.

By Terry Webb

"WITH JESUS"

One day I'll be with Jesus
My life will then begin,
For by His precious blood
Away was washed my sin.

One day I'll be with Jesus
Through all eternity,
By him I have eternal life
Because of Calvary.

Written by: Terry Webb

"ALL HAVE SINNED"

What is this you say, my friend-
You say you don't have sin?
In the light of Jesus life-
We all fall short within.

In the book of Romans, chapter-
One, Verse twenty three,
Reads how everyone has sinned-
Including you and me.

By Terry Webb

BE A STAR

Heavenly bodies known as stars, are basically like the sun-
Shining bright giving light, but differ every one,
Stars, like Holy Angels, each show a certain light-
The more power and glory, their light becomes more bright,
We can be like stars, shining bright within-
The light that we produce, will shine unto all men.

By: TERRY WEBB

"CHRISTLIKE WITH LOVE"

Through all the perils of life, we all go through,
Remember someone else, has it harder than you.
Someone today, had nothing to eat,
Praise the Lord, you had bread and meat.
There are many people with no shelter to sleep,
Praise the Lord, you have a place to keep.
Praise Him for the clothes that you wear,
For someone else, their bodies are bear.
People are homeless, with nothing thereof,
Help them my brother, be Christ like with love.

By Terry Webb

"DRY THY EYE"

We should look beyond all sorrow
Towards each blessed day,
Trust in God for He is there
To wipe all tears away.

Our day's to come shall be made glad
Our tears are not in vain,
The Lord He wants to mourn our sin
And grieve what brings Him pain.

By Terry Webb

FUTURE VIEW

Open my eyes, that I might see,
The life you have prepared for me.
The past for me, is left behind,
The future I seek, now to find.
Mistakes I've made, all in the past,
How much longer, will my heartache last.
Forgive me for the things I've done,
Teach me how to love everyone.
The hidden person within my heart,
Must now step out, and make a start.
So Lord please bring me into view,
Of a new life, I can have with you.

By Terry Webb

"FORGIVEN"

Blessed are the lives of all
Who's trespass is forgiven,
Their sins are covered by the blood
Before the sight of Heaven.

With precious blood of the Lamb
Their sins are washed away,
Their sins were purged at Calvary
when Jesus died that day.

By Terry Webb

"I SURRENDER ALL"

My times are in your hands "O" Lord-
I surrender all,
Fill me with your love and power-
Lift me from this fall.

I sank real deep in sin and shame-
Satan's schemes prevailed,
I tried to fight this fight myself-
Without You Lord I failed.

Will pain attend me all my life?
In sin, should I die?
Should sorrow be my toil and woe?
"O" Lord, please hear my cry.

Forgive me Lord for what I've done-
Hear me from afar,
Forgive the wrongs all that I did-
Heal this sinful scar.

"O" Lord, I surrender all to Thee-
To gain strength and might,
Take control, for my life is Yours-
Guide my steps upright!

By Terry Webb

"THY GRACE"

Truly, I am thankful Lord
That I can start anew,
My sins, I did confess "O" Lord"
To turn and follow You.
Your mercy is now upon me for
My sins You did atone,
Not for the labors of my hands
But Thy grace, and that alone.

By Terry Webb

"ALL TRUST IN YOU"

I know not what awaits me Lord
The future I cannot see,
Yet, I know that You are faithful Lord
To keep all harm from me.
I walk by faith, and not by sight
All trust I put in You,
You shall unclasp and set me free
With judgment just and true!

By Terry Webb

"BE THE LIGHT"

How can the world see God through us
When we still live in sin,
How can they know the way to God
When there's no light in men.

How can we say that we know God
And hate one another,
How can we not find fault in self
But criticize our brother.

If we but learn to love as God
The Father loves us all
Then we would see through eyes of love
And help when others fall

We have to bring more souls to Christ
We have to share His love
We have to try and be their guide
To Heaven high above

How many souls will come to Christ
Depends on you and me
We have to be a light to them
Through us, that they might see

Written by: Terry Webb

"CHOSEN FOR HIS GLORY"

Imagine the celebration, awaiting us one day-
When glory all in Heaven, rejoice a special way,
For Christ's completed work, in man has been done-
Accomplished there on Calvary, Christ in us has won.

He suffered humiliation, and the utmost lash of pain-
His glorious, noble prize, man's life should sustain,
We are His possession, God's glory is revealed-
Sealed by the promise, that the Holy Spirit sealed.

A Holy assembly of Saints, for all eternity-
To live a life in Heaven, forever bring free,
Chosen for that moment, of the highest praise and glory-
Through Christ we have become, chosen for His glory.

By: TERRY WEBB

"DON'T LOOK BEHIND"

We struggle with our failures, in our past life-
Our minds are occupied, with past bitter strife,
We regret half hearted efforts, reviewing till at last-
Were looking in a mirror, looking at the past.

Don't look behind, or look in review-
Always look forward, to a life anew,
Forget what lay behind, keep pressing on toward-
There is prize ahead, keep on pressing forward.

By: TERRY WEBB

"EYES OF FAITH"

Through faith we see the unseen view
Of life to come our way,
We see through faith what we must do
To guide us through each day.
If all would view through eyes of faith
Then we would see God's plan,
The mystery then would be revealed
What God has planned for man.

Written By: Terry Webb

"FOOTPRINTS OF JESUS"

Before the Lord died on the cross
He taught us how to walk,
He showed us how to live our lives
He taught us how to talk.

He said for all to follow Him
Each step that he did take,
We must follow in His footprints
Every step in which we make.

Through faith we'll see His footprints clear
Each print He left behind,
By following Him, we will find life
That some will never find.

The footprints of the Lord will lead
To Heaven's open treasure,
They will also lead our souls unto
Life, without measure . . .

By Terry Webb

"FEED MY SHEEP"

The Lord, He said to Simon Peter
Simon, does thou love Me?
Then feed my sheep and follow Me
Then I will truly see.

His words are just the same today
He say's the same to all,
He tells us all to feed His sheep
And help them when they fall.

By Terry Webb

"SIMPLE TASK 4"

A simple task, before you go to bed,
Repent all things, to the Lord overhead.

By Terry Webb

"GOD IS ALRIGHT"

The Lord of love,
The Lord of light.
The light of life,
Make all things right.

By Terry Webb

"I REPENT"

To you "O" Lord, I do repent
Thy blood is all I claim,
My sins I know, defile your word
And scorns your Holy Name.

Oh please, my Lord return to me
Your power, I once knew,
Forgive my sins that grieved Thy heart
Separating me from You.

By Terry Webb

"THE BLOOD"

My Savior died on Calvary-
His life's blood did flow,
Oh how precious is His blood-
That makes me white as snow.

The blood of Jesus Christ our Lord-
Cleanses of all sin,
"O" Lord I thank you for your blood-
That makes me pure within.

By: TERRY WEBB

"SPIRITUAL STRENGTH"

Grieve not the Holy Spirit of God
Cut not it's power source
Let the power of God flow free
Maximum strength and force

Cast down all idols and also thrones
These things to God are sin
God's Spirit then will freely flow
To give you strength within

Written By: Terry Webb

"SALVATION"

Salvation is not for sale, my friend
Salvation is for free,
The death of Christ, redemption has wrought
Salvation for you and me.
The blood of Jesus Christ, our Lord
Has obtained our redemption,
His precious blood ran down one day
To be the worlds Foundation.

By Terry Webb

LIGHT OF MY LIFE

"THE LORD IS MY LIGHT AND MY SALVATION,
WHOM SHALL I FEAR?"
He directs my path in every way,
His presence is ever near.
He's my never failing power source
For me, He is enough,
I lean on God, and rely on Him
Especially when times are rough.
I am confident that God will save me
His love always prevails,
The Lord alone is my inner strength
His love for me never fails.
All my hope, my trust and heart
I give to Thee, my God,
Who comforts me, directing my path
On every road I trod.
My God, He knows my inner fears
And keeps me from dismay,
I look to Him, and trust in Him
More and more each day.
The Lord, my light and salvation turns-
My darkness into light.
His love light shines upon my soul
MY HEART IS EVER BRIGHT!

By Terry Webb

"HOLY SPIRIT"

"O" Holy Spirit, descend on me
Through all my pulses move,
Through my weakness make me strong
All fault in me reprove.

Teach me how I ought to love
Faithful how to be,
Help me "O" Spirit, Holy and True
To be sensitive to Thee.

By Terry Webb

"HE'S ALL I NEED"

The Lord my God, he's all I need,
To make it through, this world indeed.
Each day that come, and days that go,
He strengthens me, and help me grow.
With His strong, unchanging hand,
He molds my life, to His demand.
I never want, for anything,
Under my Lord's, protecting wing.
When I hunger, my Lord does feed,
The Lord my God, is all I need.

By Terry Webb

HELP ME KNOW YOU

Make known to me Your presence Lord
With each daily walk,
Make me yield, first place to You
Help me hear you talk.
So when I hear Your voice Oh Lord
While walking along the way,
I will enjoy my walk with You
And talk with You each day.

By Terry Webb

"GOD'S GREATNESS IS SEEN"

When I look at the sky, that God has made
Filled with all His love,
The sun, the earth, even the moon
Was made by God above.

Throughout the world, his greatness is seen
Throughout the galaxy,
His greatness is seen by all His works
for all Eternity.

Written By: Terry Webb

"JESUS IS LORD"

Death it had no hold on Him
Though on the cross He died,
His spirit dwells within our hearts
Though He was crucified.

He took the keys of death from Hades
"O" death where is thy sting?
Our Savior lives and He is Lord
Jesus, Lord and King!

By Terry Webb

"NO ONE'S PERFECT"

How quick we look at others faults
And over look our own,
We paint and criticize their way's
Loudly making it known.

We need to recognize our faults
Our own hypocrisy,
Look to all through eyes of love
With hearts pure and free.

By Terry Webb

"MY FUTURE"

Though I know not what awaits me
My future I can't see,
But I know my walk will be with God
And He will be with me.

For nothing in life can satisfy
My heart and inner soul,
Therefore, I made the Lord my trust
My future to control.

Though I know not what the future brings
I'll walk with God each day,
I've put all faith and trust in God
That He may lead the way.

By Terry Webb

YOU'RE NEVER ALONE

You never cry alone, my child-
For when you cry, I do,
My child, I always share your pain-
My heart goes out to you.
although this life may bring you pain-
My child, just trust in me,
And if you will obey my Word-
I'll give you victory!

By Terry Webb

"ONCE TO DIE"

My friend, there is an appointed time
Once that you should die,
Then your inner spirit man
Will rise unto the sky.

All that you were while on this earth
All that you were within,
For in the Light of God above
You will be judged of sin.

Face to face, you will see God
As sure as mornings light,
God will judge your earthly life
With judgment just and right.

God rules as sovereign on His throne
He judges great and small,
All, who would despise His rule
Beneath His rod shall fall.

My friend abstain yourself from sin
And turn the other way,
For once your life has ended here
You will be judged that day!

By Terry Webb

"COME UNTO ME"

I am the truth, the life, the way,
Come to Me, my child and pray.
Thy burdens, I will then make light,
Thy sins, my blood, will wash them white.
Thy trust my child, put forth in Me,
For I am good, taste Me and see.
The devil has caused the strongest of all,
To take his eyes, off me and fall.
So listen to Me, my child and learn,
Make my warning, your daily concern.
Give to me, your heart this day,
That I may guide, and lead thy way.
Believe in Me, God's only Son,
I hold life's key, the only one.
"I am Jesus," and my Word's are true,
I laid down my life, just for you.
So come to Me, my child and see,
The life that I've, prepared for thee.
"I am the truth, the life, the way,
Hear my voice, My Words Obey!"

By Terry Webb

INDIVIDUALLY MADE

We are individually made-
We're all one of a kind,
No two were made the same-
We're different, even in mind.
We're made in God's own image-
To fit into His plan.
Of all creation's treasures rare-
Not one compares to man,

By Terry Webb

"NOT MINE OWN"

Within This body there lives a spirit
The body, it is not mine,
My spirit lives inside this body
On loan just for a time.

So everything that I do in life
Must be done spiritually,
To not fulfill the lust's of flesh
To live eternally.

That's why I must be careful in life
This body is just on loan,
God gave to me this body to use
Therefore it's not mine own.

By Terry Webb

"A PROMISE OF COMFORT"

A promise God has made to man
That dwell within the Lord,
His staff and rod will comfort thee
Also his shield and sword.

The Lord promised to comfort you
So whom shall you fear,
So when the wicked rise against you
Remember God is near.

Written by: Terry Webb

COME TO ME

Come to me, my precious child,
I'm ready to forgive;
Thy sins are covered in My Blood,
Come to me and live.
I am the Lord, also your God,
I've come to set you free;
My hands are outward stretched, My child,
Come now, unto Me!

By Terry Webb

"TIME OUT FOR GOD"

Tell me my friend, are you too busy
To praise the Lord today?
Are you to proud to humble yourself
On bending knees to pray?

Are you so lost in sin my friend
To do what's true and right?
Or are you ashamed in the eye's of others
By walking in God's light?

Why do you turn your back on God
When He has shown you love?
Why do you not receive from Him
His blessings from above.

Behold, with open arm's He's there
Waiting to receive,
Just open up your heart to Him
Trust Him and believe.

By Terry Webb

"I SEEK THEE LORD"

I will meditate on Your precepts Lord
On bending knees I'll pray,
My spirit thirsts for You alone
I cry to Thee each day.
Thou art the bread of life to me
Oh Lord, turn not thy face,
But fill my life with Your own joy
Touch me with Thy grace.

By Terry Webb

"ALL ARE THE SAME"

We are all one, in the eyes of God,
Although to some, it may seem odd.
Our features are the same, upon our face,
And to God, all are the same race.
For He do not love more, yellow, black or white,
Because we all are the same, in His Holy sight.
A nose, a mouth, two eyes and ears,
All experience pain, and the shedding of tears.
We're all the same, in the Lords eyes,
All created equal, under Heavens sky's.
When God made you, He also made me,
We are the same, in His eyes, you **see**.
So remember God, and His Holy name,
He looks upon man, equally the same.

By Terry Webb

"BROKEN LIVES"

A broken heart can give to life
A beauty never known,
For when that heart re-lives to Christ
It's love is clearly shown.
Broken hearts the Lord can use
Mended with His love,
Yield the fragments of your heart
And life to God above.

By Terry Webb

"CHRIST'S RETURN"

One day the Lord, He will return
To take up His elect,
The ones He call, will live with Him
The lost He will reject.

The lost are those, that live in sin
Bound they are to burn,
Prepare yourselves, for Eternity
One day Christ will return.

By Terry Webb

"FROM HEAVEN WITH LOVE"

The God who put us here on earth
Has shown the world His love,
How He has sent His only Son
From Heaven high above.

He sent His son to shed His blood
For all the human race,
He proved to all that He is love
By magnifying His grace.

By Terry Webb

"I WILL PRAISE HIM"

I will always praise my Lord and God
I will always adore His name,
I will sing aloud with a grateful heart
To Him who's always the same.

I will rejoice in the day's to come
For He will bring me there,
Under His wings I'll be always
My future He will prepare.

By Terry Webb

THY PERFECT WILL

Teach me in Thy precepts, Lord,
Thine Word, from day to day.
That I may hide them in my heart,
To honor and obey.
Cleanse my wicked heart, Dear Lord,
Please wash away my sin.
Then fill me with your precious love,
And make me whole again.
My life is yours, "O" Lord, my God,
Thine purpose to fulfill.
I give my heart and soul to you,
To do Thy perfect will.

By Terry Webb

"ALL THINGS ARE POSSIBLE"

All things are possible, through Christ-
Who strengthens you,
With the faith of a mustard seed-
He will pull you though.
The sky is the limit, therefore-
Nothing is impossible,
In the name of Jesus Christ-
All things are possible.

By Terry Webb

BE STRAIGHT WITH GOD

We are the masters, not the slaves
Of what we say and do,
Be a doer, not just a hearer
Of God's word that's true.
Be God's helper, not His neglecter
Be thou straight with God,
Keep your conscience pure and clear
In this life you trod.

By Terry Webb

"CHRIST CARES"

No one ever took the time
Or even cared for me,
There is no other friend I have
That is so kind as He.
No one else could take my sin
Then cast it in the sea,
Or lift me from the pits of hell
Or even set me free.
He gave Himself, that I may live
My life eternally,
Oh, how much He cares for me
Christ the Lord, is He.

By Terry Webb

DO YOU BELIEVE?

Do you believe that Jesus, died upon the cross?
Do you believe He gave His life, for all that are lost?
Do you believe He died, and His life was for all men?
Do you except the fact, that He died for all our sin?

Do you believe that Jesus, died and reappeared?
Do you except the testimonies, that say, He appeared?
Do you believe that Jesus, is forever always near?
There is no doubt about it, He's with you here!

By: TERRY WEBB

"FOR ALL I AM"

Please take me Lord, for all I am
Beauty hid from common sight,
For all I am, I'm Yours always
Bring me into your light.

Be merciful to me "O" Lord my God
Though my sins has grieved Thine heart,
For all I am, I repent to Thee
From sin I do depart.

For you alone can make me whole
Your source of strength divine,
For all I am, I pray to Thee
Please heal this heart of mine.

All things of earth are but a mist
That quickly fades away,
Please let me live through eternity
With You my Lord each day.

Written By: Terry Webb

FIGHT THE GOOD FIGHT

Stay within your good standards, fight the good fight,
Keep a firm stand, for the things that are right.
Everyday at work, you carry a heavy load,
But you handle it with ease, on your journey road.
Keep justice love and kindness, but walk humbly with God,
Each and everyday, on each road that you trod.
Your purpose is for guidance, also for aid,
Helping all people, in errors they have made.
But what must you do, to insure peace of mind,
Look towards Heaven, and the answer You'll find.
For all were created, by the mighty God above,
He is the answer, and the answer is love.

By Terry Webb

"SIMPLE TASK 5"

A simple little task,
To do everyday,
Keep your mind on the Lord,
Kneel to Him and pray.

By Terry Webb

"GOD ONLY KNOWS"

How can we understand "O" Lord"
That wonderful marvelous light,
Which is in Heaven, that wonderful city
Which makes that city bright.
Eyes have not seen, what You have made
Nor can we understand,
The things in which is planned for those
Who fit into your plan.

By Terry Webb

"I SEE GOD"

All around, I see the glory of God,
Everyday, on each road I trod.
I see Him in, each little child,
I see Him when, someone smile.
I see Him when, the sun is aglow,
I see Him in, the falling snow.
I see Him in, the falling rain,
Dancing against, my window pane.
I see Him in, each pretty flower,
I see Him all day, in every hour.

By Terry Webb

"THE EYES OF GOD"

The eyes of God are ten thousand times
Brighter than the sun,
So listen to me all ye saints
All evil we must shun.

The unseen eyes of God are there
No matter where you are,
The eyes of God will follow you
It matters not how far.

There is nothing that He does not see
So nothing can be hid,
All darkness shall be turned to light
All evil God forbid!

By Terry Webb

SOMEDAY WE WILL BE TOGETHER

One day, someday, we will meet in paradise,
Someday, one day, it will be very nice.
For there was one, who made a sacrifice,
He died on the cross for sin, His life was the price.
He died to save us all from sin made the devil think twice,
Jesus will come again, his chosen will meet in paradise.
I pray to be chosen, do you? It will be very nice . . .

Written by: Terry Webb

"SIMPLY TRUST"

There is no way to earn your way
To Heaven by your worth,
You cannot earn by words or works
You have to have new birth.

You must believe in Jesus Christ
Confess Him as God's Son,
Believe He died and rose again
It's all that need be done.

By Terry Webb

LET GO—LET GOD

When we put our faith in Christ
He cleanses all our sin,
If we let Him take control
Our hearts He'll dwell within.
His Spirit wants to fill us with
His blessing and His grace,
But we must let Him take control
And have His rightful place!

By Terry Webb

"HOW GREAT THOU ART"

How great thou art, who made all life
To live upon the earth,
To greatly multiply their seed
Bringing forth new birth.
How great thou art, to have a love
To always just forgive,
Each man of your creation because
You made man to live.
How great thou art for you to send
Your only Son to die,
It was all but just, part of a plan
To prove Satan, is a lie.

Written by: Terry Webb

"HIS GLORY"

All angels kneel and worship
And unto Him they sing,
Songs of great rejoicing
For He made everything.
The Alpha and the Omega
The beginning and the end,
He breathed the breath of life
giving life unto all men.
His Glory is so wonderful
Repaid only in praise,
We should honor and worship Him
All our life long days.

Written by: Terry Webb

"HE'S WAITING FOR YOU"

He gave His all, Himself he gave for us-
He gave His very life, no argue, fret, of fuss,
We belong to Him, for He created man-
Purchased us with Jesus blood, this I understand.

So we belong to Him, for now and ever more-
He's only waiting for you, to open up your door,
Behold, He is knocking, will you invite Him in-
Or do your like life better, living inside sin.

When your heart open's, He enters in your life-
You can make the choice, life or bitter strife,
He's calling out your name, do you hear His voice-
He's waiting for you, to make that special choice.

By: TERRY WEBB

"GOD'S VESSEL"

We all are just a vessel to God
Of Grace that He can use,
Just like He used the virgin Mary
It was not her choice to choose.
For those who give their lives to God
His joy, His rest they share,
Oh use me, Lord, use even me
Any time or anywhere.

By Terry Webb

"JESUS, PRINCE OF LOVE"

A love so true, to ever live,
A heart so pure, to ever give.
Something as much, as His life for a price,
He gave his life, the ultimate sacrifice.

This is true love, no one can deny,
A love far beyond, the human eye.
This special love, came from Heaven above,
Only from Jesus, The Prince of Love.

By Terry Webb

"NO OTHER NAME LIKE JESUS"

There is no other name I know
A name like Jesus,
Even still while we were sinners
Jesus died for us.

Amid the crises that life may bring
What greater help have we,
As Jesus Christ the risen Lord
Whom died for you and me.

Written By: Terry Webb

MY GOD, MY LORD

The Lord is my light, through Him I see,
He forgave my sins and set me free.
He is my God, also my Lord,
He protects me with His shield and sword.
He fight my battles, and in each war,
He comforts me, I worry no more.
He walks with me on every road I trod,
Jesus is Lord, also my God!

By Terry Webb

"WHY CALL ME LORD?"

Why call Me Lord, and don't do what I say?
Why call Me Lord, and to Me you do not pray?
Why call Me Lord, then turn the other way?
Why call me Lord, when you do things as you may?

By: TERRY WEBB

"ONE LIFE TO LIVE"

One life to live, one life to gain-
Will you reap joy, or will it be pain?
Do you love God? His precepts obey?
Or your own lusts, doing things your way:
Beware my friend, this warnings for you-
Why live in sin, why not be true,
Why pay the fare of this worlds sin-
When eternal pain is your fatal end,
You have one life, one life to gain
Will you reap joy, or will it be pain?

By: TERRY WEBB

"WHY IS CHRISTMAS"

Christmas brings much joy and cheer,
Each time it comes, once a year.
A day of love, and a day of joy,
A day when children, are blest with a toy.

A day of happiness, a day of fun,
It is the day, was born God's Son.
Unto us all, a Savior was born,
Inside a stable, He lay forlorn.

On this day, all peace stood still,
All hearts were opened, for love to fill.
A day which brought, to all assurance,
He was born, for our deliverance.

In His cradle, the little Christ lay,
His birth we call, Christmas Day.
On a very cold night, the end of December,
Was born the "CHRIST," "TO ALL REMEMBER."

By Terry Webb

"JESUS—KING OF KINGS"

On this day in a manger, laid earths new born King,
People came from near and far, with precious gifts and things.
To adore this new born Savior, to pray on bending knee,
Knowing that this Savior, will one day set men free.

Three wise men, journeyed far, to see this precious sight,
Through the desert heat of day, and through the cool of night
Guided by a light above, coming from a star,
which lead them to the manger, where the baby lay afar.

They bowed to Him in worship, and they praised His Holy name,
Knowing He will end all sin, and peace on earth remain.
These three men who bowed to Him, were very powerful Kings,
But they praised this little baby, who was Jesus—"King of Kings!"

By Terry Webb

"HOLY NIGHT"

This night was holy, love filled the air,
Peace stood still, joy everywhere.
All were endured, to one precious sight,
A new born babe, which was born this night.

Heaven was opened, with the tidings of love,
Poured upon the earth, it's love from above.
Angels came together, with a new song to sing,
Let the earth receive, their new born King.

This Lord of Lords is born, unto all men,
And He will take away, all of their sin.
He will restore, and make all things right,
And all will remember, this "HOLY NIGHT."

By Terry Webb

"A GIFT FOR THE WORLD"

God prepared for Christmas-
The gift of His Son,
Before the time earth began-
Christ would be the One.
His beloved Son Jesus-
Would provide complete expression,
God's love for His people-
Atonement for transgressions.
Unlimited is His love-
Unlimited is His giving,
Salvation for all people-
Eternal life of living.
He is the atoning sacrifice,
"A gift where unto men"
Jesus to be the Savior,
"A gift for the world of sin!"

By: TERRY WEBB

"STARLIGHTS OF THE NIGHT"

Star light, starlight's, of the night,
What makes the heavens so beautiful and bright?
They twinkle, they dazzle, so full of grace,
Lightly shinning light, upon my face.

Oh how wonderful, and so beautifully,
Those bright amazing starlight's, shinning down on me.
Each one with a story to tell with a meaning,
Gallantly shinning, yet radiantly gleaming.

Those magical, mystical, stars above,
Dance to a song, inspired by love.
Each one has a dance, all of it's own,
The power of God, through them are shown.

What beauty, those starlight's, their glory share,
Millions upon millions, are everywhere.
The magic of their glow, shines through each night,
Ever so wonderful, and ever so bright.

Oh how wonderful, and yet so beautifully,
How those starlight's of the night, shine down on me.
What makes the heavens, so beautiful and bright?
Those bright amazing starlight's, of the night.

By Terry Webb

"SUMMER"

What I like most, about what the summer bring-
Is the pretty flowers, and the birds that sing,
The joy of laughter, when the children play-
All through the summer, joy throughout their day.

While sitting in the park, under shady tress-
I like the cool air, in the summer breeze,
Nothing in the summer, that truly can't be beat-
Is the change of weather, the hot summer heat.

By: TERRY WEBB

"WONDERS OF SPRING"

Through all seasons, and what they bring,
I love it most, when it is spring.
Spring is come, and melts the snow,
Blossoms bloom, and flowers grow.
Birds all fly, out from their nest,
And all bears, wake from their rest.
Pretty flowers, their beauty show,
Soft the wind, a warm breeze blow.
Flying high, all birds fly,
Soaring through, a clear blue sky.
Warm and radiant, is the sun,
And all animals play, having lots of fun.
In the fields, they run and play,
Until night comes, ending their day.
Flowers growing, so beautifully,
Is what I enjoy, and love to see.
No other season, could ever bring,
The beautiful wonders, as of spring.

By Terry Webb

"MOTHER'S RECOGNITION"

A mothers love is very special
Our dads are seldom there,
Our mom's are always there for us
To show that someone care.

No other love compares to theirs
Except the Lord's above,
Our mom's are always reaching out
To give their touch of love.

No matter what the circumstance
No matter what's been done,
A mothers love will never change
For her daughter or her son.

Through them, God truly shows to us
The fact that there is grace,
He proves it by their tender hearts
And smiles on their sweet face.

They are always there for you
They comfort when you cry,
You can never turn their love from you
No matter how you try.

So thank the Lord for motherhood
With all their vale of tears,
Their happy moments never dim
Through all their many years.

We praise You Lord, for motherhood
And mom, to you we say,
We love you and we thank you Mom
"HAPPY MOTHER'S DAY."

By Terry Webb

'In loving memory of Cora Mae Webb'

"A MOTHER'S LOVE"

A mothers love is special
And important too;
A mothers love endures
Through all things you do.
It's something about that love
It always touch the heart;
And seems it's always there
As it was from the start.
A mother will take care
Of each precious little child;
And her love for them endures
All their life long while.
Mothers always know
For a mother knows best;
They seem to sense the trouble
Before you're put to the test.
A mothers love is endless
And yet it's not foretold;
Because her love is pure
Her heart is made of gold.
Her love light brightly shine
Each day that she live;
For every precious child
Her heart will forgive.
Only the love of God
In Heaven high above;
Can over rule the heart
Of A Mothers Precious Love!

By Terry Webb

ABOUT THE AUTHOR

Terry Webb was born in Birmingham, Alabama on January 12, 1958 to Perry and Cora Mae Webb and came to Los Angeles, California at an early age. Terry graduated from high school in 1976 then he enlisted in the army to continue his education. Later he was Honorably Medically Discharged early from the Military due to a non service related accident. Life was not the same for Terry after that. Although he found a job, the job didn't pay him enough to support his wife and son so he sold drugs on the side. The Money was good for a while but one day he was arrested and went to prison losing everything, including his wife and son. Upon the day of his parole, Terry tried desperately to put his life back together, but things for him were never the same. The streets of "Watts" became his hustle grounds and also his death trap because the drugs that he sold, he eventually became addicted to them himself. After 15 years of struggling in his addiction, going back and forth to prison, sleeping in vacant houses, abandoned cars and on the side of freeways, digging out of trash cans for scraps, at his lowest point in life, Terry turned his life over to the care of God and asked the Lord Jesus into his heart. God has been in the midst of his deepest struggles and in years time, has now restored everything and more in Terry's life that was lost in his addiction. Today, Terry is an active church member of the "CITY OF REFUGE" and "Mt CALVARY BAPTIST CHURCH" Terry doesn't do anything against the law but works with the law as a Loss Prevention Security Officer. God has also given Terry a heart of empathy and caring. With 4 years of study in Psychology and Chemical Dependency Counseling, he is also a Certified Substance Abuse Recovery Worker, Registered with the State of California. Terry has become a professional helper and demonstrates his impulse to care by going over and beyond the expectations of his role in helping others. By the grace of God, his inspirational poems are to help others who are lost so that they may be found in Christ. Terry believes that "POETRY TO GOD" will change the lives of everyone who reads it, one person at a time, and will make the world a better place for everyone to live, one day at a time . . .

"MIRROR OF MY LIFE"

It took much grace, to judge myself
My vanity was strong
I could not see the faults I made
Nor admit that I was wrong

Yes, money was my highest goal
My desire was to gain
But drugs enslaved my mind and soul
Which caused my life much pain

I hurt the ones whom loved me most
From me, they turned their face
For in their hearts they deeply knew
That death was my embrace

But at my lowest point in life
I turned to God whom knew
Just how to turn my life around
And show what I must do

He showed me how to live my life
To show no disrespect
He said I am to live for Him
Christ's life I should reflect

He said to keep in mind my past
The life I led in sin
Then guard well each step I take
Lest I go back again

He said to Keep in mind my past
The heartache and the strife
And keep in mind the mirror
The Mirror Of My Life

Written by: Terry Webb

**Look for all four Volumes Of
"POETRY TO GOD" On my web site:**

poetrytogod.org

Poetry To God
Volume 1
Lord Please Hear The Cry

Poetry To God
Volume 2
No Fault Found

Poetry To God
Volume 3
Into Thine Hands

Poetry To God
Volume 4
Prison Praise

www.ingramcontent.com/pod-product-compliance
Lightning Source LLC
Chambersburg PA
CBHW020850090426
42736CB00008B/325